Inner Paths

Compiled by the
Himalayan International Institute
of Yoga Science and Philosophy

Contributing Editors:
Sri Swami Rama
V. V. Merchant, Ph.D.
Geshe Wangyal
Munishree Chitrabhanu
Bhagwan Singh, Ph.D.

Published by
The Himalayan International Institute
of Yoga Science and Philosophy

ISBN: 0-89389-049-9
Library of Congress Catalog Card Number: 78-71672

Copyright 1979
HIMALAYAN INTERNATIONAL INSTITUTE
OF YOGA SCIENCE AND PHILOSOPHY
Honesdale, Pennsylvania 18431

Contents

Introduction

One mountain, many paths.

The mountain that modern man needs to climb is not as well-known as those scaled by members of mountaineer clubs. It is a secret mountain, a hidden mountain that few wish to scale, or even to prepare for the ascent. The mountain is the reality of man's own consciousness; the climb is a journey upward to the inner peaks without moving from place.

To scale these heights man must first slow down, for if he tries to assault this inner mountain he will only find himself breathless and discouraged. But modern man rushes through life. He sees hurry as a way of living, and his hurry with himself is reflected sadly in his daily habits—the way he drives his car, the way he eats and drinks, walks down the street, faces another weekend. Instead of experiencing life, all he experiences is his hurry. The task of living intelligently, with peace of mind and concern for others, seems to him a foolish wish from a bygone era. Now is a different time, he is told, an uneasy period of history. The solutions to his problems are always just around the corner—a better job, a promotion, moving to another section of the city, new technology, lower prices, another self-improvement book on the market. These dreams are indulged in year after year until he finally realizes that yesterday's dreams of promise, with all their vigor and excitement, have dissipated, to be replaced by fearful "insuring" against old age.

Where has the chase led? Even if the dreams were to be fulfilled, and more, would they make one immune from their consequences? Has the rush been worth the price? Am I healthier for it? Because of my struggle, do struggling people find in me a welcome refuge of trust and wisdom? Have I touched the lives of men and women who have earnestly hoped that I would linger more in their vicinity?

A sign of today's confusion is that people complain about the right things for the wrong reasons. They expect their health to improve as soon as the new drug is discovered; they expect the hours after dark to be safer when there are more laws and a stronger police force; they expect not to buy on credit as soon as they make more money. They cannot understand why health, virtue and happiness are not the result of scientific discoveries, merchandising, or legislation.

Hurry and confusion use energy, and the consumptive expenditure of energy, including human, proliferating on our planet today far exceeds the accumulated sum of entire Western civilizations of the past. The competitive demand upon natural resources is incredible. Almost without realizing it people, in their endorsement of material values, become more and more impersonal in their relationship with society. Their unthinking acceptance of quantitative goals expends their emotional and intellectual resources. A question may be asked here: Could the depletion of man's energies and the strain of modern life have a relationship to the startling increase of degenerative diseases in contemporary society? Our unbalanced, hurried living reflects the lack of an all-embracing perspective that would enable us to evaluate various life styles as well as the proper use of nature.

Man's spirit has requirements that may

not be entirely satisfied by his unthinking hurry. The failure to appreciate this fact of life prolongs the hurry and worry. Change exists, but man's constant searching for change and "new experiences" reflects a wish to escape, almost a refusal to be in touch with his spirit. To exploit the potentialities of matter without understanding the spiritual side of his nature, modern man undermines himself and confuses material progress with personal growth.

The pursuit of newness has become a dominant theme of our era. Yet people today are often overwhelmed by the unexpected changes that occur in every strata of society, for too much change evokes anxiety. People then start to question the values of continuity and preservation. If man lives by change alone, then the future looks foreboding, for not knowing what to expect, man panics into trying to make the present last as long as possible. But matter and its forms cannot last; entropy is its law. Clinging to the present newness or escaping into nostalgia only hastens the deterioration of man's hopes and plans. Why work and save for a future that guarantees its own obsolescence? People sense the need for some kind of permanence, but where can they find it amidst all the pressures for change?

The ancient traditions teach that man is more than matter. According to them, his home is essentially spirit. External changes are not enough to satisfy him, for humane living involves more than merely adjusting to society. By calling sympathetic attention to this plight of man, caught as he is between matter and spirit, change and permanence, the present authors here reveal how man can rediscover the purpose of his being. The authors point out, for instance, that permanence rather than change renews—and it may be a restoring change for modern man to learn that ancient truths are ever fresh. Unlike matter, they do not deteriorate—they are only forgotten. In fact the incredible age of these truths testifies to their indepletable vitality. The more man earnestly recognizes them for himself, the more he experiences their quickening effect upon him.

Each essay starts the reader on the inward ascent from a different base camp and follows a different route. These are ancient trails, well trodden over the centuries. Their reliability has been proven even if modern man does not have time to appreciate them. They attest to the value of permanence and restoration and, since others have successfully traveled these routes to the mountain peak, they provide an added incentive to the traveler. While there may be still other trails, here the reader has the opportunity to inspect the advantages of following those which are well mapped.

In Swami Rama's presentation of raja yoga one is introduced to the most ancient of all the trails, dating from before the Vedas. Here, one embarks on a holistic journey on which body, mind and spirit are integrally involved in awakening one's center of consciousness, thereby revealing the unseen heights of self-realization.

Dr. Merchant outlines Sri Aurobindo's unique synthesis of ancient Vedic truths for modern application, showing how the truths of East and West merge in each individual traveler's efforts to understand himself.

Next, Geshe Wangyal discloses the many-faceted insights found along the Buddhist path, showing how the development of the *bodhi*-mind leads one to universal compassion towards all forms of life.

Munishree Chitrabhanu then reveals to readers the relatively unknown path of the Jains. In a step-by-step journey the author explains the Jain approach to self-knowledge, emphasizing that one must first start with oneself in order to understand the rest of the world.

Finally, Bhagwan Singh presents the razor's edge—that path taken by the few who are not afraid to encounter the narrow ledges overlooking the abyss of utter confusion. Jnana yoga is not a common approach, and yet it is very practical for our day of manufactured illusions that only divert us further from reality.

It is our hope that these essays, taken from presentations given at the first annual International Yoga and Meditation Conference, will point out a direction to those readers who are eager to embark on the inward ascent. If they could only quietly realize that the description of these ancient paths can become a practical map for their own future, then their inward journey is already under way.

Justin O'Brien, Ph.D.
Honesdale, Pennsylvania
January 15, 1979

The Path of Raja Yoga

Sri Swami Rama

Yoga is an ancient word, found not only in yoga manuals, but even in the Vedas, the most ancient records in the library of man. Some of us vulgarize this word *yoga*, but it is found in all the great religions of the world, including Christianity. The ancient scriptures say: *Hiranya garbho yogasya vakta nanya puratanha*, meaning, "The first man, the first manifested one, was a great yogi" (one who knows about himself on all levels).

The term *raja yoga* was first used by Swami Vivekenanda, a great man who came to Chicago to attend the World Parliament of Religions in 1893. Raja means *royal*, and this yoga is called royal yoga because, unlike other systems of yoga, which are vague, this one is systematized. In it, philosophy, science and practice are combined. Here it is the duty of the teacher to impart the principles of yoga and how to practice them, not by studying yoga aphorisms and manuals, but through self-discipline and specific practices that will help you to attain the goal of yoga. My Master always said, "Do not teach any science without having experienced it. Then you will be able to warn your students. You will be able to guide them properly because you will be telling them not only what to do and the way to do it, but also that which should not be done."

According to yoga there is no such thing as sin, but there are obstacles which one must face. Raja yoga teaches you how to overcome them. The first word of the first aphorism in all systems of Indian philosophies is *atha* (there are seven main streams of Indian philosophy; the raja yoga system is one of them), and in all the systems the word *atha* has been used again and again.

Atha means *now*, implying *now, then and therefore*. It means that before you study raja yoga or apply the science of raja yoga you should prepare yourself, but Western man has no time for preparation. He wants to attain spirituality instantly, like instant coffee or tea. So many teachers therefore commit a serious mistake by not preparing their students properly.

They give them *mantras*; they give them this stand and that stand, but they do not prepare them properly, and this confuses Western minds.

There are many varieties of yoga, and all are equally respected, but many varieties can also confuse students. Truth is simple, but teachers can make it so very complicated that the poor students become confused. The raja yoga system, on the other hand, is a scientific path, and along the path there are milestones. You can watch and see how far you have come; you can watch and see how far you have to go. It is a beautiful path.

So the word *atha* explains to you the whole truth of all the great philosophies of the world. Do you know what the purpose of our life is? If you sit down quietly and calmly you will come to know that it is Self-realization. To communicate with another person you have to open your eyes, open your lips, move your limbs and express certain gestures, but to reach within you do not have to make any such effort.

The easiest way is Self-realization. The easiest way is to "know thyself," but this is an inward journey. For that, you have to learn to become an "insider," one who fathoms all the levels of life and finally realizes the source of consciousness. It is so important to be an insider, in fact, that in the monasteries of the Himalayas, when someone comes to us, we first try to understand whether this person is an insider or an outsider. We do not care how much he has studied the scriptures. Is he an insider or an outsider?

In the West, the educational system is very technical, but it leads toward the external world; it cannot lead inside. Man does not know himself, yet he wants to know the things outside himself. Patanjali, the codifier of raja yoga somewhere around 200 B.C., warns modern man that he must become aware of who he is. The foundation of the entire science of raja yoga is found in the first four *sutras* of the *Yoga Sutras* in which Patanjali says, "You are identifying yourselves with the objects of the world, forgetting your essential nature."

The moment you come to know your essential nature, do you know what happens? You become fearless. A student under the pressure of fear says, "Will I be enlightened? How long will it take for me to be enlightened? How long will it take for me to meditate?" He worries instead of meditating. This happens with everyone. It happened with me also.

My Master told me one thing, "Be free from all fears first." You are going through the procession of life. Why do you worry and bother for enlightenment? Start treading the path, and enlightenment dawns of itself. The first thing to achieve is called freedom from all fears, and it is the duty of a teacher to give you that freedom. He should enlighten you with the knowledge of the true values of life. It is your duty to prepare yourself for the teaching.

I want to clarify the relationship between you and your teacher. If the teacher instructs you selflessly for your benefit, follow him. If you do not find him selfless, and if he does not practice the ideals he preaches, do not follow him. A selfish teacher cannot communicate with his disciples truthfully. A true teacher is known by his selfless, loving behavior, for selflessness is the expression of true love. If this is missing in a spiritual relationship, then it is not spirituality and you should call it something different. A competent teacher is he who practices himself and who knows what he is teaching. See if your teacher is selfless. If he is, follow him. It is that simple.

My Master always said, "First, be an insider." Become conscious of this reality; that your life is not external only. You should learn to understand yourself, your ways, your internal states and your center of consciousness.

The basic concept of yoga psychology is to be aware of reality all the time. Otherwise you forget your essential nature and identify yourself with the objects of the world. Slowly and gradually become aware that reality is omnipresent, omnipotent and it is within you also. You cannot cut reality into pieces. That is the dualistic concept. Reality is within and without. There is only one truth, which is omnipresent and omniscient. Then where are you? I am in truth and truth is within me. I simply have to become aware, and that awareness is strengthened by constant practice.

In the beginning there are practical problems. You start becoming more egotistical when you feel that the Lord is within you; you feel that you know everything and others do not know anything. You go here and there and say, "My Master is great and other teachings are useless." These egotistical problems contract his personality, consciousness and vision, but when he sits near his teacher and listens to him attentively he resolves this problem.

Similarly, when you try to become an insider, when you start meditating and become aware of the reality within, one of the first problems which arises is that you become an introvert, and when you become introverted you either come in contact with your suppressions and depressions, or you become egotistical. This is a practical problem that all aspirants face.

The science of raja yoga teaches us not to identify with the objects of the world. We are used to seeing, to examining, to verifying things in the external world, but no one teaches us how to see and look within. It is most unfortunate. But according to raja yoga, even if you start to look within, you will have to face practical problems. When you become an introvert, you are not meditating. Not at all. You are just coming in touch with your superficial self which is full of conflicts. For instance, you may feel a lack of confidence. Fears and self-condemnation may arise, for whenever you close your eyes, what happens to you? You see yourself. You start talking to yourself.

My Master taught me something very interesting which I will never forget. I would like to repeat it again and again so that you will remember, too.

One day the ruler of a mountain state came with all his guards to see my Master. It was about eight o'clock in the morning, and I was standing outside the cave. I was perhaps fifteen or sixteen years of age.

The ruler said, "Brahmacharin, I'd like to

see your Master."

"You cannot see my Master," I replied.

So his secretary and guards came. They said, "Do you know to whom you are speaking?"

"I don't care who he is," I said.

Now, I was brought up very freely by a yogi. I was very humble with a humble person and I was very egotistical with an egotistical person. To be very frank, I did not have much knowledge. I used to imitate great yogis. The way they would sit, I also would sit, but I did not know what to do next.

Then the ruler came forward and very humbly said, "Sir, may I see your Master?"

So I said, "You are most welcome," and took him inside.

Now that man had been educated in Oxford, England, and he wanted to be like a Britisher and make polite chitchat. So he said to my Master, "Sir, you seem to be very lonesome."

My Master replied, "Yes, because you have come."

When you jabber your whole life, let me tell you that you make yourself lonely. Your favorite people make you lonely. Those whom you love, and who claim to love you, make you lonely. This is a fact. But do you know that this is not love? It is attachment. Love and attachment are two different things. Love means giving selflessly, excluding none and including all. Attachment is possessing something. In reality, it is bondage. There is a vast difference between love and attachment. Western people say, "How can you live without attachment?" Well, you can live wonderfully without attachment. You can live on love. Love and attachment are poles apart. One is the cause of freedom; the other is the cause of bondage.

In order to attain the highest state of consciousness, or *samadhi*, there is a ladder with eight rungs. It is called raja yoga or *astanga* yoga, and is set forth by Patanjali in the *Yoga Sutras*. *Astanga* means eight limbs, for there are eight rungs on the yoga ladder. The first two rungs are ten commitments—not commandments, but commitments. You do not have to be commanded to follow them by some teacher, or yogi, or great sage, or the scriptures. You should be committed to them because you know what you are doing. So first, learn to know what you are doing. Then start following. A blind follower will not arrive anywhere.

When you have started on your path, then you come in touch with two sets of commitments: *yama* and *niyama*. One set helps your communication with others, the other improves your internal being.

Be truthful, be kind, be nice, be gentle. In my childhood I learned those lofty ideals by heart, but I did not know how to practice them, for they are merely words which we use to console ourselves and others. My Master said, "You should learn No." Do not lie. Do not do that which is not to be done. Do not think that which is not good, not helpful.

So first your teacher introduces you to the real teacher within you which is called conscience, your own conscience. Then you start counseling within, "I should not do this because it is not helpful. This is creating an obstacle for me." The teacher inspires you, gives you strength—that strength which is already within you. The teacher introduces you to your own conscience and says, "My child, look within and be guided by this."

I can assure you, however, that the day you start counselling within, you will make mistakes. But so what? Life is not meant to be ruled by *don't*. You have to make mistakes, and you have to learn from your mistakes. But they should not be repeated. Otherwise confession has no meaning. "I confess. Forgive me, my Lord." And again I repeat my mistake and again

I confess. Then I do it again, and again I repeat the same thing. Great is he who learns from his own mistakes and doesn't repeat them. Not repeating is real repentence.

The *yamas* and *niyamas*, the first two rungs of the ladder, include:

Ahimsa—*Ah* means, *no. Himsa* means, *killing, hurting, harming* and *injuring.*

Satya—Not lying, not doing things against one's own conscience.

Asteya—Non-stealing or not having any thought colored by greed (which makes one selfish and egotistical).

Brahmacharya—Celibacy of mind, action and speech for monks; having control over sexual appetites for the householder.

Aparigraha—Not expecting gifts and favors from others as well as keeping the mind free from possessing things which belong to others.

Saucha—Cleanliness of both body and mind.

Santosha—Contentment. One of the greatest virtues. Once you have done your duties you should learn to be content with the fruits you receive therefrom.

Tapas—Not to allow the senses to contact the objects of the world and create obstacles on the path of spirituality. Senses dissipate the mind, and when the mind is dissipated you cannot attend to work properly.

Swadhyaya—Study of the sayings of great sages and study of the scriptures as taught by Self-realized and competent teachers. Study of one's own internal states, actions and speech.

Ishwara Pranidhana—To be aware of the reality, to witness the center of consciousness within. To surrender the individual soul before the cosmic one, or to expand the consciousness into cosmic consciousness.

The ten commitments of yoga science prepare you to communicate with people outside and to be composed, to be tranquil within. Then you start doing your work, start treading the path within, from gross to subtle, to the subtlest center of your being.

The third rung of the ladder of raja yoga is *asana* or posture. There are two sets of postures in yoga—physical postures and meditative postures. The student prepares himself for meditation with a posture which should be easy, very comfortable and at the same time, steady. The Bible explains it concisely in the passage, "Be still and know that I am God." I have visited many monasteries around the world, and some of them do not understand the meditational method, but in the Bible it is clearly written that the student should first learn to be still.

Pranayama, or control of the breath, is the next rung of the ladder. Once the student begins to work with himself, his awareness turns inward immediately, and he becomes aware of his breath. The study of breath is a very interesting subject. The Gita explains that there are two guards in the city of life called inhalation and exhalation, that create a bridge between the body and the mind. As long as they function, it is called living here. When they cease functioning, that is called death.

"Learned is he who understands the mystery of life here and hereafter." When you start studying your breath (not only through practicing breathing exercises, but also through being aware of the whole concept of breath), you wonder, "Who is supplying this life breath to me?"

There is only one center that supplies this life breath to you; there is only one father; there is only one proprietor of all these bodies. When a yogi becomes consciously aware of this fact he does not hate anyone. His consciousness establishes itself in the Self of all, and this knowledge of equality flows uninterruptedly. He becomes aware of oneness with the cosmic center who supplies breath to all. You cannot live without breath. You are freely receiving that life breath all the time. But the subject of *prana* is different from and deeper than the science of breath. Here, it is enough to say that there is a direct link between you, the individual, and the cosmic reality that supplies life breath to you. That's why the first thing that the raja yoga and Zen Buddhist traditions teach their students is breath awareness.

Once you become aware of your breathing process you will find irregularities in it. But by practicing specific methods of breathing, or *pranayama*, you can gain conscious control over the unconscious activities of the autonomic nervous system and eliminate these irregularities.

Breathing is closely connected to the mind. You might ask the question, "How is breathing connected to my thinking process?" I can easily tell you. If you suddenly tell me shocking news, for example, I will experience jerks in my breath. The motion of my lungs will be disturbed. My right vagus nerve, my autonomic nervous system, and my heart and brain behavior will all be disturbed. My pulse rate will increase. For this reason breath is a thermometer between the body and the mind which registers both physical and mental conditions. This is a science in itself. It has its philosophy which is not known through books. Only the yogis who practice it traditionally know this science deeply. *Pranayama* is a complex subject.

But even if you have studied your breath, you will realize that you are not only body and breath. You are more than that. You are a thinking being. In Sanskrit there is a word which you also find in English, *man*. It is called *mana* in Sanskrit, *mind*. It means that you are not merely a body; you are a thinking being as well. So your thinking process should be under your control. You should learn that all the modifications of the mind can be brought under conscious control, as Patanjali tells us, and the last four rungs of the raja yoga ladder are devoted to this end.

You can learn to control your mind very well—because it is yours, but do not try to control the minds of others and make them dependent. When one becomes dependent, one suffers, so you should learn to be independent, and you should not make others dependent upon you.

When you have learned not to identify yourself with the objects of the world, and when you have perfect control over your mind and its modifications, then you realize your true Self,

for control means to gather together the dissipated forces of the mind and to become creative
and dynamic. Control does not mean suppression
or repression.

What will happen when you have control
over your mind and its modifications? Can you
imagine? Your personality is transformed, but
you do not become abnormal. Patanjali is very
direct and truthful about this. He says, "Then
you will be established in your own essential
nature." Once you have known your true nature,
the center of consciousness within from which
consciousness flows in various degrees and on
various levels, you are enlightened. To dispel
the darkness of ignorance and attain freedom
from all suffering is the philosophy of raja yoga.
You can do this when you have control of the
mind and its modifications.

You are the architect of your spiritual
life. You should learn to build it. Be brave. The
brave alone enjoy the world. Learn to enjoy the
world by living here and now. The first word of
the first aphorism of Patanjali's *sutras* tells you
to be here and now.

When Patanjali talks of the withdrawal of
the senses, the fifth rung of the ladder, he does
not mean that you should withdraw yourself
from the world. Instead, you should make all

your actions spiritual and change your attitudes and living patterns. Patanjali's system is followed by both householders and monks.

Raja yoga says that you should learn to understand your whole being. You are a nucleus and the universe is your expansion; you have to know the nucleus first, and then you'll know the expansion. The relationship of man with the universe will be easily understood after attaining *samadhi*, or union with the absolute reality.

When you start trying to gather yourself together you will find yourself so dissipated that you don't have the faculty of decisiveness. This is why it is very foolish for teachers to say that concentration is not necessary. If you cannot concentrate, can you do anything efficiently? Your speech will be different from your thinking. You will walk in a different direction from where you want to go. If you cannot concentrate on a book, how can you read and understand it properly? It is foolish to say that concentration is not necessary; that is escapism, persuasion and exploitation. Concentration is a marvelous technique, to be developed gradually and gently. It will make you dynamic in your daily life in the external world.

Patanjali explains various ways of concentration. When concentration strengthens spontaneously, it flows toward the object of meditation, and when meditation strengthens, it leads to *samadhi*, the ultimate rung to be achieved by a student of raja yoga. There are various stages of *samadhi*, but after one has attained the first stage he is no longer in the bondage of misery and pain.

Some students think that without practicing the preliminary steps of raja yoga they can attain samadhi, but that is not true. No matter which *mantra* you have, if your technique is defective, if you do not have a philosophy of life behind it, that technique alone will make you a technologist, but not a meditator. Work with yourself gently. As you look after your body, look after your mind. Proper meditation is very useful, and raja yoga teaches that.

Once you start doing meditation, you will come to know that life consists of more than merely learning. You talk of learning. You say, "I want to learn, I want to learn." But that is not the proper attitude. There is something higher. On the spiritual path un-learning is much more important than so-called learning. What you really need to learn is "un-learning," but only in meditation will you discover what this means.

I wish you could forget everything. If

you could forget all that you have learned, in which language would you talk to yourself? What would be your state of mind? Do you know that when you have unlearned all the languages in which your mind thinks, you attain the state of *samadhi*?

With the help of meditation and through the un-learning process, you will come in touch with your unconscious. Gradual and systematic meditation will enable you to make your mind one-pointed and will give you the power to penetrate the infinite library of intuitive knowledge. Then you will attain the state of real joy and happiness. Joy is realized by only that mind which can fathom the deeper levels of peace. One who has attained such an equilibrium of mind is never disturbed by worldly fetters because he has learned how to remain undisturbed, how to live here and now. He has learned to be here, yet above. If we live only here, we are flattened like a ball of clay and cannot get up, so we should learn to live here and yet remain above.

You know who is in *samadhi*? He who has no more questions. If you do not have any questions, if all your questions are solved, you are in *samadhi*, but as long as your mind is busy with dialogues, that is duality. If one part of your mind puts a question and another part answers it, you are not in *samadhi*. The day you are free from the argumentations of the mind, you are in *samadhi*. *Samadhi* is strengthened when you learn to practice your meditation constantly, without any interruption. This final rung of raja yoga has led you to become the most practical of persons, for now you are fully free, in full awareness of reality.

The Philosophy of Sri Aurobindo

V. V. Merchant, Ph.D.

Sri Aurobindo's voice has been heard in many quarters, for he was a poet, philosopher, revolutionary, scholar, humanist, educator and, above all, a seeker of truth. But what is it that is unique about the philosophy of Sri Aurobindo?

Perhaps in the year 2001 we will have a conference of yoga and meditation on the moon, in the following year on Mars, then on Jupiter and then on Venus. These expectations, through the process of supramentalization that Sri Aurobindo envisions, are within our reach—if not in our lifetime, then in the lifetime of future generations. We may yet be there on all those planets and galactic places, not only in outer space, but also in inner space as well as on our earth. We will see the Auroville that he envisioned—a new international City of Dawn, of truth and of the future—a living reality in the architectural design of all the planets and galaxies, made up of mathematical forms that have spiritual significance.

In his own words, let Sri Aurobindo describe what he has come here to give us:

> Our aim is not, either, to found a religion or a school of philosophy or a school of yoga, but to create a ground of spiritual growth and experience and a way which will bring down a greater Truth beyond the mind but not inaccessible to the human soul and consciousness. All can pass who are drawn to the Truth, whether they are from India or elsewhere, from the East or from the West.

The reason I wanted to bring out the significance of this particular message of Sri Aurobindo is that modern man has become very suspicious of philosophy and religion. Reform movements all over the world have become as much suspect as politics. I am speaking of the conventional, traditional reform movements involving those philosophical and religious factions that have arisen from many, many streams. In their original intent they started out with a great deal of intensity in their search for truth, in their quest for man's identity. But somewhere along the way confusion reigned. From the hippie and the yippie movements, pop art and op art, the drug scene, psychedelics, and what not, we have gone through many "isms," cycles and phases.

Now if we were to ask the questions, "Who is the truly modern man?" and "Is he modern because he happens to live in the twentieth century in a chronological age?" The answer of Sri Aurobindo is, "No." The truly modern man is one who has bridged the gap between the past, the present and the future, who has brought consciousness to bear on them, and who has built isomorphs between himself and his world. The modern man is one who has found his way to truth and realization through consciousness and who is aware, irrespective of the time, the geographical locale, or the spatio-temporal reality he lives in.

The truly modern man is the conscious man, no matter when he lives, whether it be the 6th century B.C. or in the 20th century A.D., Sri Aurobindo has a special appeal for modern man because his teachings offer a new hope for mankind, a message of joy and promise for the future, for the possibilities of mankind. His teachings meet the longing of the human heart for a truth that integrates all the wonders of outer and inner life and eliminates the restrictions that cause false education and hence the sorrows of the world.

Sri Aurobindo's message in this sense is

universal and archetypal; it works and appeals through the individual, the modern man of our day and age who is aspiring for higher consciousness, but who is still the representative of his own age. His message opens new soul doors, a new consciousness to direct and inspire our lives, not only at a metaphysical level, but in every aspect of our lives, even amid the mundane things of our life.

In Sri Aurobindo's philosophy no aspect of human existence, whether it is physical, vital, emotional, aesthetic, intellectual, or spiritual, is avoided, overlooked or shunned. He tells us that true knowledge, therefore, is:

> . . . not only Science, but Art, not only book knowledge, and information, but growth in culture and character are parts of a true education; to help the individual to develop his capacities; to help in forming of thinkers and creators and men of vision and action of the future, this is a part of its work.[1]

You may wonder, how I came in contact with Sri Aurobindo, and why is it that I felt this deep need to study, as I have done, Sri Aurobindo's works. When I was a little girl, about three years old, I was passing by a bookstore where I first saw a picture of Sri Aurobindo. Later, I saw a copy of *The Life Divine* with the same picture on that book. As I was passing that bookstore with my mother I told her that I wanted that book. And she said, "Now why in the world would you want that?"

But I said, "I want that book."

She said, "You just had a book. You had a birthday. You can't have everything that you want in this life."

So we went home, and my mother thought that after two or three days I would forget about that face and about that book. Then I reminded my mother that I wanted that book again. And she said, "You can't have it."

So I went on a hunger strike. I told her that I was not going to eat. She said, "When you are hungry, you will eat. I'm not going to get you the book."

So I did not eat for three days, and at that time at the end of the day my mother came to me in tears and said, "I cannot bear for you to do this to me. Let's go and fetch your book."

Since then Sri Aurobindo and the works of the Mother and their living spirit, have become a living reality in my life. Eight years ago I met with an almost fatal auto accident. I met with this experience—my rendezvous with death—and was almost in the twilight zone and ready to leave this body when I heard the voices of Sri Aurobindo and the Mother telling me to stay in the body, that my work was not done—that I had to stay in the body to finish that work. That is why I had to come here. We had to meet; that, too, has a significance.

Sri Aurobindo was born on August 15, 1872. The Independence of India falls on August 15, 1947. The birthday of Sri Aurobindo was chosen to give India's freedom a vaster significance and a more intensified purpose for its spiritual destiny. In this regard, Sri Aurobindo pointed out this spiritual destiny when he was asked to give a message on the 15th of August, 1949, in addition to the message he gave in 1947. He addressed it primarily, but not exclusively; to the West, its import is for all mankind.

He said in this message that the body and soul of mankind, in the East and in the West, have remained separated for too long. There was no reason for man not to marshal the energies of the divine body, he felt, to make the body a fit instrument for spiritual growth, not only through hatha yoga, not only through raja yoga, but through an integral development of the individual and the collective life of man. He proceeds:

> East and West have the same human nature, a common human destiny, the same aspiration after a greater perfection, the same seeking after something higher than itself, something towards which inwardly and even outwardly we move.

There has been a tendency in some minds to dwell on the spirituality or mysticism of the East and the materialism of the West. But the West has had no less than the East its spiritual seekings and though not in such profusion, its saints and sages and mystics. The East has had its materialistic tendencies, its material splendours, its similar or identical dealings with life and matter and the world in which we live. East and West have always met and mixed more or less closely. They have powerfully influenced each other, and at the present day are under an increasing compulsion of Nature and Fate to do so more than ever before . . . There is a common hope, a common destiny, both spiritual and material, for which both are needed as co-workers.

One of the reasons that Sri Aurobindo's philosophy is extremely apropos to modern man is because he represents the consummate genius, the highest synthesis, of the best values and ideals of both the East and the West.

At the early age of seven his father, who was a physician, wanted to remove him from any Indian influence. This was when India was a slave nation, under the rule of Britain, so he sent him abroad to get a Western education. From the ages of seven through twenty-one, Sri Aurobindo stayed in England and had the best of English education at Cambridge. He was at the top in all his classes, distinguished himself very brilliantly and was rated among the greatest scholars. During this time he learned Latin, Greek and French and studied the best of classical and European literature as well. By the age of fourteen he had composed poetry in several languages. During his later education, he also mastered German, Italian and several other languages.

But when he came back to the soil of India he felt empty and incomplete. There was a part of his education that had still not been rounded off. So he plunged into the depths of Indian spirituality, and no one has delved into, explored and investigated the profundity of this spirituality more deeply than Sri Aurobindo. As a result, he certainly ranks among those who started the process of East-West understanding and integration and gave man a dynamic and an integral vision at what the East and West can do together, through uniting rather than dividing or separating.

Continuing further in his 1949 address, he points out:

> It is no longer towards division and difference that we should turn our minds, but on unity, union, even oneness, necessary for the pursuit and realization of a common ideal. The destiny and goal, the fulfillment, towards which nature, in her beginning obscurely set out and which she must, in an increasing light of knowledge, replacing her first ignorance, constantly persevere.

But what shall be that ideal and that goal? That depends on our conception of the realities of life, and the supreme reality.

Sri Aurobindo gives us another unique insight when he discusses the human body. In more ancient philosophies and religions the emphasis is on shunning, or deriding, the body, considering it to be an obstacle. Because this is difficult, these traditions promoted a great deal of pessimism and emphasis on escape from the world. In Sri Aurobindo's philosophy, however, the body is divinized until the last cell, the last nerve and fiber respond in joy to the light of the divine. And until this transformation of the body comes through, "to work with the body is to pray for the divine," as the Mother says. Therefore the body also has a place in Sri Aurobindo's schema as an important instrumentality, and must not be ignored. The body does not go away, the body does not give up its demands just because we think it will, because we do not like Freud, or because we are afraid of our desires, their persistence and their wrong movements.

Another of the more unique things that Sri Aurobindo teaches is about creating and transforming our earth life. In this connection he speaks of two movements of consciousness for man: the ascent and the descent of consciousness.

The ascent of consciousness he explains as the core of evolution from matter to life, to mind, to supermind. In traditional philosophy, only the curve or evolution as the ascent of consciousness is important. In Sri Aurobindo's philosophy the descent of consciousness is equally important. This bi-polar, reciprocal movement allows the divine to enter into our daily lives through supermind. Thus the mental levels, the illumined and inspired mind, the vital nature of man, the physical nature of man, even the material nature of man must be transformed through the power of the descent of consciousness. He called this process the involution of consciousness.

"Only that which is involved can evolve," says Sri Aurobindo. And you will know how true this is even in our daily lives. In this sense we have to take into account that there has been an increasing divergence between the tendencies of the East and the West. "The highest truth," as Sri Aurobindo points out, "is the Truth of the Spirit, a supreme truth about the world, and yet imminent in the world and in all that exists."

The West has placed its faith in science and machinery, in economics, in social, political and other institutions. Sri Aurobindo reiterates that until we realize that evolution (as well as the growth of these institutions of science and machinery) is founded in the spirit, that same machinery, that same material science man has created, will devour him. And therefore the

> . . . science of the West has discovered evolution as the secret of life and its process in this material world. But it has laid more stress on the growth of form and species than on the growth of consciousness; even consciousness has been regarded as an incident, and not the whole secret of the meaning of the evolution. An evolution has been admitted by certain minds in the East, certain philosophies and scriptures, but there the sense has been the growth of the soul through developing of successive forms through many lives of individuals to his own highest reality. For if there is a conscious being in the form, that being can hardly be a temporary phenomenon of consciousness, it must be a soul fulfilling itself and this fulfillment can only take place if there is a return of the soul to earth in many successive lives, in many successive bodies . . . .
>
> The ascent of the human soul to the supreme spirit is the soul's highest aim and necessity for that is the supreme reality; but there can be too the descent of the spirit and its powers into the world and that would justify the existence of the material world also, giving it a deeper meaning, a divine purpose to the creation, and solve its riddle.
>
> East and West could be reconciled in the pursuit of the highest and largest ideals, spirit embrace matter, and matter find its own true reality and hidden reality in all things of the spirit.[2]

For Sri Aurobindo philosophy is not merely a quest of the aspirant for the truth of things of the intellect only. It is also the endeavor to realize the truth in the inner self as well as in the outer life. Although he did not like to consider himself a philosopher, he was undoubtedly a greater *dharmatma* than a mere *darshanik*. But Sri Aurobindo represents the finest and best qualities of both, in spite of himself!

Looking through the large spectrum of three hundred works that he has left behind, one is amazed to consider how many pages a day he must have written, and for how many years. The deep wisdom that he poured out in these books has imprinted itself in the *akashik* records as well as concretely for us to learn from and be inspired by.

Apart from his spiritual experience, what has he given to the realm of philosophy, ethics and humanities? "Aurobindo's treatises are among the most important works of our time in these fields. Sri Aurobindo himself is one of the greatest living sages of our time," says Dr. Pitirim A. Sorokin, of Harvard University. But apart from his contribution in ethics, philosophy, religion, humanities, sociology, psychology of man, politics, poetry—there is one other thing Sri Aurobindo tells modern man. It is about something that modern man cannot live without:

money.

Sri Aurobindo says, "Money in its true origin comes from the divine."[3] Therefore the truly divine person should not shun money but must make wise use of it, must conquer the forces that rule money (which are necessary for the perfection of the outer life of man) and rededicate them back to the origin and source from which the money comes. You will find in most traditional philosophies that money is shunned, money is detested and looked down upon as the source of all evil. But Sri Aurobindo reiterates that money in itself is only a means. Most of those who possess it are possessed by it rather than having it as their possession. And so until modern man becomes a trustee of the funds that he uses, he will find that he will remain a slave to it. Therefore money assumes, in Sri Aurobindo's philosophy, a spiritual significance; it must be used for purposes, for functions, for such activities which deepen, heighten and widen the consciousness so that it will dedicate it and offer it back to the divine.

The more one reflects on the present condition of man and his existential predicament—the presence of dread and despair—the more it seems that Sri Aurobindo's poignant description of the dilemma of the rational,

materialistic man of today is imminently accur-
ate. In effect, man is leading himself into a
catacomb, a labyrinth where he is no longer sure
of anything, least of all the clue to the riddle of
his life and the riddle of the world. Man acclaims
and yet derides the prospect of a divine harmony. This existential predicament of the
modern man in search of a soul, caught in the
throes of rational materialism, experimentalism,
behaviorism, extremes of empiricism or material
science, is very acutely and aptly expressed in
Sri Aurobindo's own words, a verse from *Savitri*,
his modern epic, in which he says:

> He has no certain light by which to work,
> He seeks himself and from himself he runs,
> Always he journeys, but nowhere arrives . . .
> An idiot hour destroys what centuries made.

Alas, reliance on the sceptic intellect has
become a blind obsession with us moderns. We
have grown purblind and myopic. We can no
longer even grope our way to the soul's last
heaven of bliss and harmony, love and light. In
this connection Sri Aurobindo reflects,

> Reason was the helper;
> Reason is the bar; . . .
> Effort was the helper;
> Effort is the bar; . . .
> Desire was the helper;
> Desire is the bar; . . .
> Ego was the helper;
> Ego is the bar. [4]

What then is the solution for modern man?
Says Sri Aurobindo:

> If thou shouldst have humanity advance, buffet
> all preconceived ideas, thought thus smitten
> awakes and becomes creative. Otherwise it rests
> in a mechanical repetition and mistakes that for
> its right activity.[5]

The question is:

> What is there new that we have yet to accom-
> plish? Love, for as yet we have only accomplished
> hatred and self-pleasing; knowledge, for as yet
> we have only accomplished error and perception
> and conceiving; bliss, for as yet we have only
> accomplished pleasure and pain and indifference;
> power, for as yet we have only accomplished
> birth and growth and dying; unity, for as yet we
> have only accomplished war and association . . .
> In a word, godhead: to remake ourselves in the
> divine image.[6]

In his book *The Destiny of Man*[7], Sri
Aurobindo's vision of humanity is that of
supramentalization. Here he speaks of humanity,
of the future, of the supramental race of man.
Mind you, this has nothing to do with the concept of the superman of Nietzsche. The real
superman, or the supramental race of man, is a
spiritual race of man, Sri Aurobindo points out.
He discusses here, in this particular volume, the
future of food, sex and the new means of procreation, and the destiny of the body.[8] Would
man be able to survive if he were to take his
nourishment only from the elements, as once

the sages of the Vedic and Upanishadic ages were able to do? Will he always have to go through the process, the physical-biochemical process that we know as eating, digesting, elimination, etc.?

He also raises the question, in this particular section, on the future of sex. Will man always have to go through the same physical act in the process of creation, or will he be able to create through other methods of conception?

He also points out here that God is multi-faceted. He observes,

> We may speak of the Supreme as if He were a mathematician working out a cosmic sum in numbers like a thinker resolving by experiment a problem in relations of principles and the balance of forces; but also we should speak of Him as if He were a lover, a musician of the universal and particular harmonies, a child, a poet. The side of thought is not enough; the side of delight too must be entirely grasped: Ideas, Forces, Existences, Principles are hollow moulds unless they are filled with the breath of God's delight.[9]

It is no accident that Sri Aurobindo was sent down to us from on high to show us the way out of the crisis of our age, to lead us to the core of truth and deliver us from the trammels of the ego, the body, the senses and their objects, the mind, and the spirit. Sri Aurobindo has brought to man a new way of looking at life, a new vision embracing past, present and future. He has helped to prepare the ground for fuller manifestation of the transforming power of the divine in the great process of evolution.

Finally, let me give you just one line from *Savitri*, a modern epic, the great odyssey of the spirit of Sri Aurobindo, in which he says, "All can be done if the God touch is there." With this God touch the supramentalized race of men will be a possibility in the future, and my hope is that the work of transformation has already begun. The prime necessity is that each individual shall discover the spirit, the divine reality within, and express that in his being and living.

References

1. From Vasant V. Merchant's article on "Education and the Significance of Life." *New Outlook Magazine*, Jan., 1964, p. 24.
2. From *Messages of Sri Aurobindo and the Mother*, 2nd series, pp. 19-23. Sri Aurobindo Ashram Press, Pondicherry, India.
3. For further elucidation on this theme, refer to the book *The Mother* by Sri Aurobindo, 1969 edition, Ch. IV, pp. 14-19, Sri Aurobindo Ashram Press, Pondicherry, India.
4. *Thoughts and Glimpses* by Sri Aurobindo, 1964 edition, Sri Aurobindo Ashram Press, Pondicherry, India, p. 3.
5. *Ibid.*, p. 4.
6. *Ibid.*, pp. 5-6.
7. *The Destiny of Man*, compiled from the writings of Sri Aurobindo and the Mother, 1969 edition, Sri Aurobindo Press, Pondicherry, India. Refer to Section Four, "The Divine Superman," pp. 178-180; Section Five, "Supermind and Humanity," pp. 183-189.
8. *Ibid.* Refer to "Destiny of the Body," pp. 190-201, "The Future of Food," pp. 202-204, "Sex and New Means of Procreation," pp. 205-209.
9. *Thoughts and Glimpses* by Sri Aurobindo, 1964 edition, Sri Aurobindo Ashram Press, Pondicherry, India, p. 7.

Buddhist Teachings for Modern Man

Geshe Wangyal

In the Buddhist tradition there are two prayers for taking refuge in the Three Jewels. The first prayer is in Sanskrit and the second in Tibetan.

> *Namo Buddham Saranam Gacchami.*
> *Namo Dharmam Saranam Gacchami.*
> *Namo Sangham Saranam Gacchami.*

I bow down and go for refuge to the Buddha.
I bow down and go for refuge to the *Dharma*.
I bow down and go for refuge to the *Sangha*.

> *Lama dang gon chock rim bo chay nam*
> *pa coon la chak tsel Shing gyab su chic.*

I bow down and go for refuge to the Lama and the Three Precious Jewels.

It is very important to recite a prayer for taking refuge, even for those who do not believe in the teachings of the Buddha. There is great benefit in hearing it, great benefit in contemplating it, and great benefit in meditating on it. Therefore, I give you these prayers to the Three Jewels. Whatever I have to tell you is from the Buddha's word and the commentaries written by the great Indian pandits and Tibetan scholars. The ideas are not my own. Nor can I mention everything here. What I shall say is only a drop from the great ocean of the Buddha's teaching.

I have spent many years of my life studying in Tibet. The lamas with whom I have studied often began their discourses with verses like this one. These are the words of Tsong-kha-pa, the great reformer of Buddhism in Tibet:

> This life which has leisure
> Is more precious than a Wishing-Jewel;
> So difficult to find, it is as quickly gone as
>   lightning in the sky.
> Thus realize that all worldly activities
> Are like chaff in the wind,
> And seize the essence of leisure and opportunity
>   day and night.

I would also like to quote a verse from the *Bodhicarayavatara*, or *Entering the Bodhisattva's Deeds*, by the famous Indian pandit, Shantideva. The subject is the same as that of the above verse, but the meaning is slightly different.

We have obtained this life of leisure
   and opportunity,
So difficult to find, and able to achieve man's
   purpose.
If we do not make use of this life,
How can we actually obtain this opportunity
   again?

This life of leisure and opportunity is extremely useful and important if one wishes to gain enlightenment. It is more valuable than a great treasure of diamonds, rubies, emeralds and other rare jewels. Why is it so priceless? If we use it properly we can obtain the perfect enlightenment of Buddhahood because the greatest treasure—the cause of Buddhahood—exists within us. It is hidden within our minds. No ordinary person can see it. It can never lose its potential of producing the great omniscience of enlightenment, and by using our life properly we can increasingly develop this treasure until it culminates in Buddhahood. For this reason great lamas like Tsong-kha-pa and Shantideva mention first the importance of a life of leisure and opportunity in all their discourses.

Perhaps I should now explain what I mean by the Tibetan word *lama*. *Lama* can be translated as *none superior*. He is the Buddha, *Dharma* and *Sangha*. To show the importance of the *lama* I named our monastery in New

Jersey, "Lamaist Buddhist Monastery." There are some misleading explanations of the term *lamaism*, based on early investigations of Tibetan Buddhism; therefore some scholars dislike using the term. However, I feel that it refers to the important practice of relying upon the power and teaching of the *lama*, who is the Buddha. The Buddha can also be called the *lama*, for there is no one superior to him, and his followers in India certainly called him a *guru*, the Sanskrit equivalent of *lama*. Therefore I thought it important to use the word *lamaist* in our monastery's name.

The Buddha was a great yogi. He devoted himself exclusively to yoga for six years before he attained perfect enlightenment, and after that he taught that through yoga and meditation we could finally attain our purpose— Buddhahood—just as he had done. He gave many diverse teachings to help us attain that goal, but they all can be divided into the teachings on abandoning non-virtuous deeds and the teachings on taking up the practice of virtuous deeds. Ordinary people tend to commit non-virtuous acts and not to accumulate merit. In order to resolve this problem, the Indian pandits, as well as the Tibetan scholars and lamas, wrote many books on generating *bodhi*-mind, the humanitarian mind which is the highest antidote to non-virtue.

Bodhi-mind is the wish to attain perfect enlightenment for the sake of all sentient beings. This wish directs us along the right path, the one which leads to the final goal—Buddhahood. *Bodhi*-mind encompasses all sentient beings, for the Buddha taught that all sentient beings— animals, great sinners, and so on—will one day be delivered from the misery of *samskara* and will attain Buddhahood. Some Western authors say that this wish also encompasses trees and grass, which are not sentient, but non-sentient objects cannot attain Buddhahood.

To attain Buddhahood requires great effort. Although the potential to become a Buddha is always with us, there are many obstacles to block the way to that goal. Though among us there may be some who are already enlightened, most of us are not. First we have to purify ourselves of defilements caused by our previous non-virtuous deeds, and to clear away these defilements we must generate *bodhi*-mind.

How do we actually generate *bodhi*-mind within ourselves? It is difficult for an ordinary person to produce it at once, for *bodhi*-mind is the mind of compassion and loving kindness towards all living beings. To generate it we must

understand that all living beings have been our
mothers, fathers, sisters and brothers, since we
have been born in all forms of life from begin-
ningless time. In our present life, because of our
previous non-virtuous deeds, we do not recog-
nize these living beings as our close relatives and
friends. Furthermore, as a result of our egoism,
we are attracted to one person, feeling, "He is
my friend," and reject another, feeling, "He is
my enemy." Selfishly cherishing our own lives
makes it impossible for us to cooperate with
others and produces disagreements. But by
understanding first that all beings have been our
relatives, we can more readily feel compassion
and loving kindness towards them, and we can
subsequently produce *bodhi*-mind. In this way
bodhi-mind becomes the greatest antidote to
our selfishness.

Buddha Shakyamuni gave many different
teachings in accordance with the different
capacities of his many thousands of disciples.
Yet all his teachings had the same purpose—to
help all living beings to deliver themselves from
the misery of *samskara*. He knew how to teach
deliverance to everyone. He was the most able
teacher of teachers, god of gods. The Buddha's
followers are still practicing all of his diverse
teachings. They fall into two divisions: the

Hinayana, or "lower vehicle" teachings, and the Mahayana, or "higher vehicle" teachings. In order to attain the final goal—Buddhahood—we must practice the teachings of the higher vehicle, but we must avoid discriminating against any of the Buddha's teachings, saying, "This is high" or, "That is low." All these teachings are the highest. The Buddha taught only that which each disciple needed to ripen his understanding of reality. Therefore it is crucial to realize that all the teachings have the same purpose, differing only in accord with the capacities of the disciples. The teachings are like sugared water— from whichever side of the cup you drink, the taste is always sweet. Some scholars express this idea in a simile using salt water and the ocean, but I think sugared water is more appropriate.

Buddha Shakyamuni clearly understood the disposition and capacity of his listeners. When many thousands of people are gathered together to listen to one speaker, they have many different reactions: some feel, "Oh, that's not correct," and others think, "That's excellent." When the Buddha's many disciples asked questions, the Buddha answered them all with one word, and each understood clearly according to his own capacity: such is the excellence of a Buddha. However, this great variety of teachings sometimes confused later followers so when the teachings were transmitted to Tibet the great Indian Pandit, Atisha, unified them, proving them non-contradictory.

In Tibet we respect the teachings of such great Indian pandits as Nagarjuna, Asanga and Chandrakirti just as if they were the word of Buddha Shakyamuni. However, their varied teachings are arranged into two distinct schools of tenets—the Hinayana tenets and the Mahayana tenets. In addition, there are two main Mahayana systems: the Madhyamika and the Vijnanavada, and there are two main Hinayana systems: the Sautrantika and the Vaibhashika. All of these systems have subdivisions, and Tibetan scholars consider that the teachings of all of them are important for practice, as they all lead their followers toward the right path of liberation from *samskara*. Thus the Buddha told his disciples, "I have shown you the way to deliver yourselves from the misery of *samskara*. You should know that your deliverance depends upon your own effort."

Refuge in the Buddha, *Dharma* and *Sangha* is the entrance to all these teachings. Therefore, I remembered the prayer for taking refuge at the beginning.

Q: How does Buddhism view Christianity and Jesus Christ?

A: Our books do not mention Jesus Christ specifically, but many non-Buddhist and worldly gods are mentioned directly. Buddha himself said that he would manifest in the form of non-Buddhist gods to help others. He appears in whatever form is helpful to living beings. Therefore I accept that Jesus Christ can be one of these manifestations of the Buddha.

Q: What is the status of Buddhism in Tibet today?

A: As you know, since 1951 from seventy-five to eighty thousand Tibetans have left Tibet for India. Through the kindness of His Holiness the Dalai Lama, they are practicing their religion even more strongly than before. Nowadays, His Holiness is still working very hard, though his situation is different. In Tibet, he was very removed and difficult to meet, but today he is much more accessible. We do not have much news about Tibet, but I do not think there is any religious practice in that country now.

Q: When you left Tibet were most of the

*"tablets" taken out? Are they now with Bud-
dhists outside the country or did they have to
be left in Tibet?*

A: Some of them were brought out before the
arrival of the Chinese communists. Nowadays
the Tibetans are bringing them together and
reprinting them. They are even being collected
in Western countries. I brought some books with
me, including some works of Tsong-kha-pa and
some of the great Indian pandits.

*Q: You said that the Buddha answered thou-
sands of questions with just one word. What
was that one word?*

A: It can be any kind of word. It is always correct because it fulfills each questioner's wish.
Whatever is asked, the Buddha's answer is clearly
understood. This is a characteristic of the great
knowledge of the Buddha.

*Q: Can you give any specific techniques to
develop bodhi-mind?*

A: For modern man the best technique is to
first hear about the benefits that come from
generating *bodhi*-mind, for this is the only means

by which we can attain perfect enlightenment. Ultimately we will all reach Buddhahood. Although there are many kinds of practices (such as renunciation and the right view of voidness), only by practicing *bodhi*-mind can we attain Buddhahood. We should practice it towards everyone, and toward animals. Once it arises spontaneously in our minds we will be the sons of the Buddha. Even the poorest person who practices it will be an object of veneration: the gods will bow down at his feet. This is taught in the *Bodhicaryavatara* by Shantideva. When we face trouble we will have nothing to fear, neither demerit nor defilement of passion. When one has this mind it is like being in the company of a hero.

> *Dak gi jee nyay sak pa gay wa di*
> *Ten dang dro wa kun la gang pen dang*
> *Khyay par Jetsun Losang Drak Pa yi*
> *Ten pay nying bo ring du sell jay shoke.*

> Whatever virtue I have accumulated,
> May it benefit all living beings, and the
>   teaching,
> In particular, may it clarify for a long time
> The essence of the teaching of the
>   Reverend Tsong-kha-pa.

The Philosophy of Jainism

Munishree Chitrabhanu

The day dawns only to those who are awake. Those who are asleep, slumbering and covering themselves with blankets, do not enjoy the beautiful sunrise. In the same way, those who are covered with ignorance, confusion, egotism and desires are not able to experience the divinity which is every moment trying and striving to unfold within each of us.

Once my teacher mentioned that man is running in all directions, trying to find God. But ultimately, when he is exhausted and gives up everything and sits quietly in peace of mind, then he finds that God has been in search of man. Though this may seem a humorous paradox, yet it contains a very deep truth.

We hurry in a hundred directions. We want to have power. We want to have miracles. We want to have this and that. And the main thing for which we are born, we don't want. And what happens? The indweller of man is watching us. "I want to talk to man," says God, "but he is running. When I go here, he goes there. When I go there, he runs in another direction. He is not quiet."

God does not talk to a person who is in a hurry, or restless, or engulfed with many desires and many kinds of ego trips. When he is quiet, then God whispers. His truth comes in such a quiet way. Whenever I meditate, when I am calm, then I feel this more and more, deeper and deeper.

Today I am going to talk to you about Jain philosophy. Philosophy means, "love for thinking." We have love for everything, but when love for thinking increases, then a person becomes a philosopher. He wants to know why he or she is on this earth. What has he come to achieve? What to gain? What is his own aim, and what is his own relationship to the universe?

When a person opens the window, looks at the universe and starts thinking, at that moment the person becomes a philosopher. He looks toward the vast universe, and watches himself, and tries to understand the nature of his relationship to this universe. When he is not clouded with ignorance, when he is not covered with many expectations and lower kinds of motivations, then his perception is clear. In that moment of clarity, insight starts coming. And when insight starts coming, he realizes that the microcosm strives to reveal the nature of the macrocosm. The self tries to reveal the nature of the higher self.

In that moment of clarity of insight man's journey starts. So far, his life has not been a journey towards anything. It has been a wandering; it has been a circling. Mobility alone is not direction; movement does not necessarily mean that it leads to any goal. From the moment he gets the insight, however, that what he has been searching for outside is within, waiting to use the beautiful things which are hidden in him— from that moment, he has direction.

Yoga means "yoke." Practicing yoga, you yoke your awareness and your thinking to yourself so that you will be able to use your latent potential and all your hidden energy. Each of us is made up of infinite energy of which we are not conscious because of our limitations. But when we break the limitations and reach that state of calmness, we feel the surge of energy. It has many beautiful names. Some call it the energy of *kundalini*, others name it *shakti*. There are so many words for it, but they all indicate that hidden power within each of us. Yet the power does not come unless you experience purity of mind and the state of calmness of meditation.

The teacher helps you to become quiet and calm and to be free from your ego trip, and in that moment when you reach your Self, your natural energy flows out. The teacher is only an instrument to help you open your door. It would have opened of itself if you had been living naturally, but you don't have any faith in yourselves. You are always thinking, "Somebody must come and open my door," because you don't understand what you are.

As the child, seeing his mother, becomes calm even though the mother gives nothing but her presence, so a person who goes near the teacher, near any god, near any beautiful shrine or temple, becomes calm at that time. So some people say, "When I was in Mecca, I received inspiration." Hindus believe that if they go to Benares they will be inspired. Others go to Israel and say, "Oh, I saw the light of God descending on me!" Some go to Jerusalem and testify. Some say, "I was near my *guru* and I felt the light." In different places, in the same way, people have these insights. Do you think the light comes from the stone at Mecca or the water of the Ganges or the cities of Israel or from the teacher?

If these experiences come to one they can come to all. Those who do not have faith in any particular place, and who do not become quiet in that place will not receive anything. They will see a beautiful shrine as merely a stone, or an archeological monument, or the image of a person. Only those people who seek with tranquility and confidence and faith will quiet down their minds and find the answer. They calm down, they surrender themselves, they are free from the ego. In that moment of calmness, the door opens. Many people don't believe in themselves so they say that a savior or *guru* has opened the door, and they see themselves as merely an instrument. But in reality they have come to their own place, and this is why they received what they wanted.

Three steps are mentioned in Jain philosophy. The first step is to be yourself. As long as you are not with yourself, you will be running in all directions, projecting many different things. When you see a person you have a prejudice against, you project your negative feeling. When you see a person whom you love, you think he or she will give something to you. As long as you are fluctuating and unbalanced, you won't be able to reach yourself. So the first step is to be yourself. When you are becoming and being yourself, then you come to your real nature. We are called human beings, so our nature is *being*. If we are not being, then we are not human beings.

Just to be is the most difficult accomplishment. Just to be. It is easy to shout and make all kinds of noise. It is easy to recite a hundred *mantras*. But to sit quietly for ten minutes without allowing any talk or thought is very difficult. Your mind will bring a hundred thoughts, and your body will start jumping.

I have found in my life that many things are easy. I walked thousands of miles. It was easy. If somebody gives me a compliment, I don't say anything, and this is not difficult. The difficulty is just to be. Once I had the craze to write the name of God, so I wrote nine *lakh mantras. Lakh* means a hundred thousand. So nine-hundred-thousand names I wrote in a craze. But it was easy because my hand was writing and my mind was doing its own business. To chant is easy. The whole body chants while the mind can do a hundred crazy things. It does not require any tranquility and balance.

In the laboratory of my life I have found that these things are not difficult. They appear difficult as long as you have not done them, but as soon as you start doing them, you will realize they are easy. The mind has little to do with them, so it can do its own business at the same time. But to be yourself, to be with yourself, brings an explosion; then see where your mind goes. What kind of thoughts does it bring? In that moment you will realize that everything is under your control—except your mind.

You can control the whole world, yet not be able to control your own mind. The greatest achievement is to bring the mind to the center, to the point of tranquility. Then the change starts working, and you start changing yourself from within. You cannot help but begin to change yourself because when you are in your center you see rubbish. You see the garbage and what is unclean. You see all that you don't want. But eventually you see everything afresh and anew.

Shakti doesn't come from outside. We are *shakti*. Power does not come from outside. We are power. Power is not the energy that works outside. It is not the energy that works through you. It is the energy itself. We are energy.

In Bombay there was an old man who was sick. Once his son came and asked me to visit him and give him some consolation and blessings because he was not able to move. I went and saw two nurses helping him because he was so weak that he could not get up without their help. A month later I asked his son, "How is he?" And his son said, "He is in the same condition. There is no improvement."

The very next day there was a fire in the building. The old man was staying on the seventh floor and there was no servant to help him or elevator to bring him down. But would you believe that this old, helpless man was the first one to climb down the stairs! He got up and ran out of the door. He did not wait for any nurses or any relatives to save him. When I heard this, it was very difficult to believe. The person who could not get up without two people's help, got up and climbed down seven stories.

What we call *shakti*, the power or energy, is hidden here in us, my friends. But we don't believe it, and that's why we spend the whole of our lives moving restlessly in circles. This is our *shakti*, what the ancient seers called the *kundalini shakti*.

One spark of this shakti which is hidden in you can create the whole human being. That is our *shakti*. My teacher used to say, "Do you know that I am the product of one small seed, one small sperm? If these sperm are properly used for growth and for creation, you will find a hundred teachers in you. But if you use this *shakti* for pleasure, for temporary joy, your enlightenment will be dissipated. Enlightenment comes when we realize the power of each sperm or each drop of this *shakti*. In this *shakti* is a human being. Each of us is holding this power, and we realize this when we come to our center.

The first principle in Jainism is *atma*. *Atma* means *soul*. When *atma* knows himself, he becomes *Paramatma*. When he knows himself he is God. In Hindi we have other words for this process. *Jiva* becomes *shiva* and *Kankar becomes shankar*. *Kankar* means *a small stone*, and *Shankar* means *the God*. *Atma* means *soul* and *Paramatma* means *supreme soul*. *Jiva* means *soul* and *Shiva* means *God*. Thus *jiva* becomes *Shiva, Kankar* becomes *Shankar, atma* becomes *Paramatma*.

This ability to change, to realize our Self is our original capacity, and that is our greatest treasure. The whole of Indian thinking is not built on anything but what is revealed from within: and this is that the nature of the macrocosm can be found in that of the microcosm. This is the first and most important discovery for mankind: to know that he is holding the macrocosmic potentiality in this small microcosm.

From the moment he realizes that, he is no longer a small, wishy-washy human being. He is divine. And the first step you must take is to be yourself.

Then be yourself and what happens? The second step is see yourself. To see, you have to be. If you are not in a state of being, you cannot be in a state of seeing. We may see everything around us, but we don't see our own selves. This has become a very painful situation for mankind. He sees everything, but he does not see himself. But when you start to be yourself, then the next step comes and you see yourself.

The first and main *sutra* given by Mahavira is called *ege aiya* in the *Acharanga Sutra*. The meaning is, "see only your soul." The verse is, *Egum jane, savum jane*, which means, "know yourself and you will know the universe." Know the I, and you will know God. If you know the nature of gold, you know all the golden ornaments of the world because they are all made from the gold. If you know the nature of clay you will know all the pots in the world, because all the pots are made from the clay. That is why at first we start from ourselves, and we say, "What is my nature?"

Herman Hesse, who wrote *Siddhartha*, coined a new word. He was not happy with the old word *philosophy*, so he coined a new word, *philossia*. Philosophy means *love of thinking*. Now Hesse talks about *love of seeing*, for *sia* means *see*. Thinking is not enough because one can think without seeing. One can spin through the whole world without seeing oneself. We want to have the love of seeing ourselves, and then we know what we really are, what our inner nature is and how we can reveal that nature and build a relationship between the self and the world.

How do we start? The Jain tradition has given us four qualities to develop. The first is amity, or *maitri*, a surge of love. It has no reason. You do not feel it because somebody has given you something; you feel the nature of yourself— love. If you give a piece of bread to a dog, he will follow you; he will lick your feet. That is not love because it is an exchange. If you wait for somebody to give you something or to thank you, or favor you, and you say, "Oh, I love you," that is a bargain. It is not love be- cause he or she gives and you have to show your appreciation. On the other hand, if they do not give to you, you may say, "Oh, who cares for them? Let them go to hell!" Do you think you will go to heaven while they are going to hell? It is not possible. We are all in the same boat.

When you see yourself in your real light, that is amity. Do you have this amity, the feeling of friendship, with all? No? Then start with yourself. There are people who are friends with all the world, except themselves. They do such dangerous things to themselves, such heinous things to themselves, and they destroy their own souls with their own skills and their own minds.

In the Gita, which is Hindu, as well as in the *Dhammapada* of Buddhism and in the *Uttra Dhyan Sutra* of Jainism, in these three beautiful books is found the same message. They all say be your own friends in slightly different ways: your soul is your friend and your enemy is yourself. That's why you lift yourself with your Self. Don't destroy yourself with yourself.

It is difficult to understand that there is no outside enemy. How can we destroy ourselves with ourselves? What can we destroy? You have all seen the suicide of people who go on drinking too much, using energy in sex too much, who are loaded with negative thoughts. Day in and day out they are destroying themselves. It is a suicidal tendency. You call them intelligent, and some are very big executives, but they are destroying themselves.

So first, we have to be a friend to ourselves. It is good to take a little time and ask,

"Do I do anything by which I destroy myself?" Start the day with that. Then when you go into the world you will take the things that help your soul rather than harm it. You will not take any bad thoughts, or bad actions upon yourself because you know that by identifying with bad thoughts you are destroying yourself. Putting a bad apple in a basket of good apples causes the good apples to rot. So you say, "No, let that thought go out."

Once we accept a bad thought it is difficult to remove it, for it enters very deeply. So be yourself, and then see yourself. This is the first step in creating amity toward yourself, and when you have amity for yourself, naturally you have amity for all. A person who does not harm himself or herself is not going to harm anybody else, for in order to harm somebody, one has to harm himself first. Think of a matchstick. When the matchstick tries to ignite something, first it must burn its own face; it is not going to burn others if it does not first burn itself. In our life also, before we harm others we harm ourselves.

Now your journey is beginning. A person who is living on a *maitri* level feels his energy flowing; it is coming up because this is love. There is no hindrance, there is no obstacle, there is no power causing the energy to stop. It is flowing when we take the step of amity.

When you have amity, then the second quality to develop is *pramoda*: appreciation. Appreciation means to see your own good points, your own good qualities, and to see the same qualities in others. Find some good quality in anybody you see, and tell them about it. Show appreciation. Why do you look for the bad thoughts, the bad things in the person? See that each human being has some good quality. That is why the human being is surviving. As soon as that last good quality is gone, the person will be gone.

One of the principles of Jainism is *anekantavada*, meaning that each object, each person has many facets. A diamond, for instance, has many facets, many aspects, many dimensions, and each dimension represents something different. Jainism is not a religion that emphasizes its own exclusive truth. All the religions of the world make one whole truth. When you talk about one, another is missing. You cannot say, "He is my father," and at the same time say, "He is the son of my grandfather." This second aspect remains unspoken, or implicit. In the same way the many facets of the reality of truth cannot be spoken of simultaneously.

When we realize this we start seeing the

good things in everybody. This is *pramod*,
meaning that your heart is full with a sense of
appreciation. See something good in each human
being, and you will start loving all people. Then
your relationships with the world will be so
beautiful that when you part from the world,
you will love everybody, you will have no hatred
toward anybody. Because you have seen something good in everybody, you will have no
enemy. And when there is no enemy you are
free from this cycle of birth and death.

It is the animosity, the wrong desires for
somebody which causes you to take rebirth.
This is the *tanna* that causes you to come back.
When you don't have any kind of feeling of
negation, then you are never bound, and you do
not have to come back to the world. So this
way, the quality to develop is the sense of
appreciation.

In that also you have to begin with yourself. You say, "I am not only a human body.
In the center of this human body there is a
quality which is ever-existent, blissful and is consciousness itself. That which is consciousness,
ever-existent and blissful, that is me."

What you see in yourself is going to become evident in you. If you see yourself as a
rotten piece of dung, as a nothing or nobody,

then that will become evident. So please, respect yourself because you are carrying a beautiful quality in you. You are carrying *Paramatma* in you. If you don't respect yourself, who is going to respect you? And when you respect yourself, the world will respect you. The world is nothing but the echo of your own voice, and that comes from within.

The inner light is not in a hurry; it is not in a rush. I see two kinds of rat-race. There is a rat-race for material things, and there is a second rat-race for miracles. You say, "Oh, I want to get enlightenment in two minutes. Hurry up, and we will become enlightened." How? Without purifying? Without cleansing? Without distilling yourself? Without removing negative qualities and activities? How can you become enlightened if you are not pure?

The law of the universe is purity. From kerosene you make gasoline, and from gasoline you make spirits. It is pure. As long as that substance is impure, you call it kerosene because there are a lot of impurities in it. When it is purified, you call it gasoline. When you purify it still further, it becomes spirits. And it goes on purifying. So before we reach enlightenment we have to distill our essence. After a great deal of distilling, what remains is pure. That is enlightenment. When dross has been separated, what remains is pure, intrinsic gold. You are not making intrinsic gold. The gold was always there, but it was mixed with the dross, but when you remove the dross, you have the gold. You see this in you, and then you see it in others.

The third quality to develop is compassion. *Karuna*. You have a feeling of compassion for those who are suffering. You don't wish for any private salvation, and you don't try to run away. Your heart is like a mirror which reflects the pain of others. When you have *karuna*, then you also have the fourth quality, *madhyasta*, which is equanimity, or equilibrium. Pain and pleasure come. In pleasure there is no need to jump around, to be over-exuberant, and in pain, there is no need to go downhill or to be overwhelmed. You have a balance under all conditions.

These four qualities come when you see yourself. So the first step is, be yourself. The second step is, see yourself. You see yourself in the light of amity, appreciation, compassion and equanimity. Then, when you have taken these two steps, the third step is to free yourself. Be yourself, see yourself, free yourself. You are free. Nothing is binding you because these four beautiful qualities have freed you from your inner bondage. And when the inner bondage is broken, outer bondage is broken, too.

So, the Jain philosophy emphasizes inner unfoldment. It says again and again, "Realize this energy within." The energy is striving to blossom, but this will happen only to those who are alive. Those who have deadened their consciousness with ignorance, hate, egotism and greed, for them the stirrings of knowledge have no meaning. So we have to purify ourselves, to open ourselves. Then the *atma* becomes *Paramatma*; the qualities of the soul unfold to reveal the flower of the pure Self.

I pray that your quest will be fulfilled by realizing your inner nectar. It is there. By being yourself and seeing yourself, you will be able to free yourself.

The Concept of Consciousness accor~ding to Jnana Yoga

Bhagwan Singh, Ph.D.

The topic that I have been asked to discuss is "The Concept of Consciousness According To Jnana Yoga." The term *consciousness* is used here as a cognate word for *self (atman* or *purusha)* the knowledge *(jnana)* of which is considered the ultimate step to the highest end, emancipation *(moksha)*. Self-knowledge *(atman-jnana)* is considered to be the way to it. This subject is rather complex and difficult. There is a lot of literature on it, both in the ancient classical philosophical sources of Indian philosophy as well as in recent writings in modern languages. Many popular writings, even, present the specifically Vedanta view of consciousness and knowledge to the Western audience. Although they have served the purpose of making esoteric doctrines available to seeking people, they have also created many false myths and misconceptions. So I shall try here to clarify the concept of consciousness briefly and make a few comments on jnana yoga as the way to enlightenment—the ultimate value.

One of the distinguishing features of Indian philosophy in general is that, "throughout its long history, it has consistently given the foremost place to values."[1] In the Upanishads the problem of self-knowledge has received almost exclusive attention. They speak, for example, of the final goal of life, the means to its attainment and the inner peace and joy which signifies it, more often than on "knowing" or "being" as such. Value realization inspires their philosophic investigation as a whole.[2]

All seekers want and need to attain knowledge for enlightenment, and yoga is a way to that. In one sense, jnana (knowledge) is the prime goal of everyone, and unless we fall a victim of separation by holding that hatha yoga, mantra yoga, tantra yoga, bhakti yoga and karma yoga, etc. are mutually exclusive, we do not have to miss the point that the ultimate goal of all yoga is knowledge. It is this knowledge that brings about *mukti, moksha, nirvana* or *kaivalya*, (liberation, emancipation or freedom). The question arises—emancipation, liberation or freedom from what? And what is the nature of the consciousness that is free? And which yoga leads to it? Probably because some writers and teachers have been misunderstood, an impression is created that Vedanta yoga is the only jnana yoga. The fact is that in the long and complex tradition of India, Vedanta is but one system of philosophy. Knowledge is the goal of Sankhya yoga too. Outside the traditional Vedic schools, the final goal of Buddhism, i.e., enlightenment *(nirvana)* is also attained by knowledge. Jainism uses the term *kaivalya jnana* as the cause or source of final release. So jnana is the goal of several Indian philosophical systems, including both the theistic systems that believe in God, and the non-theistic systems as well. Jnana is the knowledge that brings about ultimate freedom. However, the nature of the subject of that knowledge is given different semantic designations: some call it *atman* and others call it *purusha*, some call it soul *(jiva)*, others term it no-soul *(anatta)*. Some call it *sunya*, and others use some other term. Let us call it "X." Part of the confusion is sometimes semantic, and the use of the same or similar terms by different schools, not always clearly distinguishing the terms used, has led to serious ambiguities.

In the title of this essay the word

consciousness is used in a special sense. But
consciousness in general can be of many kinds,
and there are many meanings of it. If consciousness in the sense of *atman* or *purusha* or the Self
is to be freed, what is it to be freed from? One
of the basic concepts used in this context is that
of *avidya*, or ignorance; thus it is freedom from
ignorance. Under this term is included ignorance
of all different kinds. When one does not know
and understand his or her own body, mind, soul
or spirit, sometimes these words and everything
else are used ambiguously and interchangeably,
and one is said to be in bondage and suffering.

What is this *avidya*? It is *avidya* when we
do not know what is "me." Pronouns me, you,
I, we, he and she, etc., are used for that "X," or,
better still, these pronouns are particular values
of "X," considered to be variables. Different
traditions give it different names. When we do
not understand what we are and mistake the
Self for something else, we suffer. Each one of
us may have been troubled by one or another
kind of emotional or psychological problem,
only to realize later that it was unnecessary and
that we should have known better. We all try
to know and understand life, and that is the one
thing that eludes us.[3] Yoga is a way to that end,
for through yoga we can understand life,

ourselves and our roles in it without being led away by complex and eluding life situations. In this way we are able to lead our lives better. That can be done only if we understand, and such an understanding, or knowledge, is really the goal of jnana yoga.

In daily life, we go from one routine to another as though we were in a "rat race" or a "squirrel cage," and nothing seems to be making any sense. Then, we take a retreat or go on a vacation, hoping that the problem will be forgotten or overcome. But the problem of *samskara* and *maya* follows us there too. There is no vacation from life. That problem is resolved only when we understand or know it, and thus we know the Self.[4] All the different practical methods of yoga are geared to that end. The problem arises when one confuses Self, consciousness or soul, in this sense, with something it is not, and there arises a conflict of roles, or a split-personality. Several kinds of trouble and suffering arise because of ego conflicts or malfunctions of the ego.

Those who have realized at least that they need to know are better off than those who do not know that they don't know, and/or do not know that they need to know. Further, in yogic knowledge there is a "functional blending,"

or a "putting together," of body, mind, breathing and all other vital functions.[5] In fact, by
natural necessity every human being has to do
yoga, and does do it, whether he is conscious of
it or not. Even animals, in trying to realize their
goals, keep their body in a proper position or in
a certain posture, and control their breath at
times. They concentrate, and only then do they
succeed. A holistic discipline, harnessing all our
energies in a unitary way, is yoga. Certain practices of hatha yoga are a necessary step in that
direction.

Hatha yoga is sometimes taken to be taking care of bodily activities only. But those who
hold that hatha yoga is not related to raja yoga
or that raja yoga is not related to jnana yoga are
really not aware of the fact that none of these is
exclusive; they cannot be completely separated
from the others.[6] They are all one. They all
function as a unity. There is a difference in emphasis only. Which path one follows depends at
what point of development one is, whether or
not one understands what the Self is. If one
does understand this, then all conflicts are resolved. If one does not, then more effort is
needed for the attainment of that knowledge.
Vedanta *(advaita)* jnana yoga, makes it very
explicit that the essential non-dualistic nature

of the universe has to be realized; otherwise there is no possibility of true emancipation.[7]

Some swamis and gurus, in their popular descriptions of yoga, have sometimes misdefined the nature of consciousness and have taken it to be some kind of a substance only. They hold it, for example, to be one kind of substance as opposed to another (i.e., it is "mind"; it is not "matter"). Or they may consider consciousness to be cognate with spirit, and that it can live and function by itself, without any relation to the body or the brain. Here again, the term *mind* or *consciousness* is being used in a very specific sense.

The nature of consciousness as *atman* can be best understood by taking an illustration from the Upanishads.[8] There are several states of consciousness (i.e., waking, dreaming and deep sleep). What is the nature of the common witness *(sakshi)*, the "X" factor in all these states? Let us consider these different states. All of us spend a lot of time in the waking state. We enjoy or suffer, depending on the nature of the objects experienced. There are a lot of objects that we see, feel, hear, think or imagine. Thus, there is objective consciousness when we know a lot of objects. What about that aspect which we call "I"? How much do we know about that? Do we ever get the pure "X" that is "me" in the waking state? No. In the waking state we are always conscious of "X" plus something, "X" plus some title of me. The last name and the titles that go along with being an Indian or an American or white or black, or social security number, or the titles of a grandfather or father or mother—all these are called titles.[9] We are conscious of "X" with titles during waking life. This waking state in life is not only enjoyable and/or frustrating, it is probably the longest and most important period in our experience. Our most important decisions and other actions belong to this state. Thus, in the waking state we enjoy and suffer an objective consciousness as well as a subjective consciousness resulting from our titles. Whether or not that mental consciousness (*chittavritti*) is pleasant or unpleasant, it is definitely tension-giving. Let us remember, then, that there is the "X" plus a consciousness of the titles and the objects during the waking state.

The waking state is not the only kind of experience that we have, however. What happens during the dreaming state? There are several psychological theories about dreams. Here, however, we are concerned only with the nature of the subject and the objects from the angle of consciousness. During the dreaming state, again, there is objective consciousness as well as the consciousness of titles. We experience objects that are pleasant or unpleasant, i.e., a nightmare or a sweet dream. And in either case it is a tension-giving experience. Similarly, there is an experience of dreaming of oneself, for example, as a prince riding on an elephant or as someone running in a desert being chased by a rattlesnake. In other words there is again a consciousness of "X" plus titles, plus objects and, depending on their nature, the experience is either pleasant or unpleasant and generates a certain kind of tension.

The third state of deep, dreamless sleep is in certain respects very different from these two. In that case we are not dreaming, at least we are not conscious that we are dreaming, and we are not awake. We are not conscious of either titles or objects. There the tension of objective or subjective consciousness is absent in that state. The tension that comes because of the ego, or subjective consciousness of titles, is also absent. That is at least one reason why deep, dreamless sleep is so relaxing and the waking up after it is so invigorating. Whatever is called "X," or pure "I," or "me," is not absent in that state. It is very much there, because when we wake up we say, "I had a very nice sleep." That sleep was relaxing and invigorating because of the absence of tension caused by subjective consciousness and the different kinds of objects.

A question was raised in the Upanishadic times about the possibility of there being another state in which the objective consciousness is suspended, and the subjective title consciousness also suspended, but one in which the person is neither unconscious nor asleep as in the case of deep, dreamless sleep—a state in which the brain and the nervous system are not asleep. They are working, but not quite in the same way as in the deep sleep state. They are not benumbed, so to speak, by sleep. This state is called *turiya*. Can one be in such a state consciously? The answer is yes. It is possible for any one of us to be in that state. Quite naturally, because of the absence of the consciousness of objects and the attendant reactions, this state will be infinitely more invigorating and relaxing than deep sleep. In this state one will not be conscious of one's ego and titles by which we are defined in the waking state and determined in the dreaming state. What remains is that "X" which is a common witness of all the different states that one experiences. The "X" was there during the waking state; that "X" was there during the dreaming state; that "X" was there during the *turiya* state. That "X" is that witness *(sakshi)* then, that is called *chidmatra*[10] in the Upanishads. Literally translated it is "mere consciousness" as "witness."

It can be safely said, then, that you are at least that. I will not totally endorse what Vedanta seems to hold when it says that "one is only that" in reality and that everything else about one is mere superimposition.[11] One could not be considered a conscious, living human person, in my opinion, if one did not have the body and all its functions. One could be that alone only in the abstract sense. It is this "X" or this consciousness that is called *purusha* in Sankhya philosophy and *atman* by Vedantins. Let us call it Self. When one is face to face with it, figuratively speaking, when one meets the lion in its own den, one encounters that Self.

A question may be asked, Who is encountering what in that state of *turiya*? Actually, nobody is encountering anything. It's just a state of being—the state of being one's Self. It is in this sense that the Upanishads declare, "That thou art," That I am." That, which is called "the consciousness" in Vedanta, is also termed *sat-chit-ananda*, the being, the existence, the consciousness and the bliss.[12] But this bliss is not within the limits of the pleasure-pain principle. It is altogether different, qualitatively. The experience of the Self is not a consciousness of any sensory pleasure. One suspends the sensuous consciousness. It is not in any way a sensory experience in the ordinary sense of external sense experience. The full realization of the Self is the *jnana* which is the final goal of yoga. One realizes then what one is when his consciousness is completely freed and liberated from the limitations of subjective as well as objective consciousness of either ego titles or objects. If you realize that, you can say easily, "Oh! That's where my ego cheated me. I took myself to be 'this,' but I am only 'that'."

I have heard from a non-Cartesian that we are not what we think, but we are what we do. I will say, not only are we not what we think, in that respect, but we are also not what we do. The mere witness as such is no doer, either. It becomes a doer only in association with the ego and the mind-body complex. In one respect we are what we think or what we do, and in that context whatever we do determines to a great extent what we shall be. Yet it is possible for us to detach, or non-attach, ourselves and watch the whole drama: How our own ego deludes us, how our own intellect cheats us, and how our mind makes a fool of us!

How sometimes our own thoughts misguide us, and we act like fools! Yet we all love that foolishness. We are deluded by *maya*, and yet we love it. But *maya* is not to be totally rejected while we are in it, anyway. We can only learn the way to deal with it and not be deluded by it. Abandonment of *maya* is the wrong attitude. An interpretation sometimes taken by misguided Vedantins says, "It is all *maya*; don't talk about it. We have to get rid of *maya*, leave the world of *maya*." If that is literally what they mean, then where will they go? Is there any other place? Other misguided Vedantins say *atman* will go to some other world." Is there any other world in the ultimate sense in Vedanta jnana yoga? No! There is only one world and all the multiplicity in it is said to be *maya*. Real knowledge consists in understanding it, in order to transcend it and to free oneself from its bondage. There is no "world" of *maya* after one realizes its true nature.[13] The realized person, having knowledge, learns to live according to the enlightened way. The ultimate subject is free. The realization of that true nature of one's self, without any admixture of adventitious qualities, characteristics, or titles is what is called the realization of *jnana*, or *atman*.

In the yoga tradition very important

distinctions are made. It is the understanding of these distinctions that leads to the knowledge called discriminative knowledge.[14] There is *prana*, that is, the life-breath; there is mind, that is, *manas*, the internal organ of feeling; there is ego, that is, *ahamkara*, the I-making consciousness; there is body. All of these function through the nervous system. It is you, the *purusha* or *atman* as the Self, who is the charioteer of the chariot of the body and the driver of the sensory-motor apparatus.[15] If you are able to lead that chariot through the life-world successfully, knowing what you are doing and why you are doing it, then you are a self-realized person. But if you do not have that realization, even though you may be earning a lot of money by teaching yoga exercises, or preaching about it, you are not a *jnani* (enlightened) in the highest sense of the term. You may be a great teacher of raja yoga in all its aspects, but if you do not have the knowledge, you are not a fully emancipated or liberated person.

Jnana means knowing in the sense of realization and understanding. This realization and understanding is actually a direct experiential knowledge in which knowing and being are one and inseparable. It cannot be known deductively or inductively. It cannot be attained through any indirect method of knowing or through direct sensory perception. The saying is, "How can the seer be seen?"[16] How can one think about or even talk about the unthinkable? Yet we think that we must find a way to talk about it. The trouble is that as soon as we start talking about it, semantic and linguistic problems and difficulties arise. Yet this knowledge can be experientially discovered and understood. It is *jnana*.

Some call this knowledge, mystical, and hence the use of the word, "mysticism." This has been understood from two opposite points of view: Some Western philosophers have dismissed all philosophies of India in the past, partly because of what may be called the "myth of mysticism."[17] This view is that all Indian philosophies are of a piece, characterized by a certain obscurantism that makes them inaccessible to clear statement and thus invulnerable to criticism. The different yogic philosophies are first lumped together and then dismissed as impenetrable nonsense. The fact is that the philosophies of yoga are multiple and diverse, and they have been subjected to mutual criticism as well as criticism by other schools of philosophy. If a certain experience described in the traditional vocabulary and terminology remains obscure, it is very likely due to the inherent inadequacy and limitation of expression. It is not justified on that account to dismiss it as unphilosophical. On the other hand, there are those who glorify the so-called mystical element. Some of them even try to hide their own confusion and unclarity, and in that sense their ignorance *(avidya)*, by glorifying inexplicable, or mystical, experience. The fact is that the knowledge attained through jnana yoga is clear and unambiguous. There are only degrees of ignorance. If there is anything that is not clear, it is still ignorance. *Jnana* is quite unadulterated. There is no mystery in it or about it. It is mysterious only so long as one does not understand it.

Some writers claim that all mystical knowledge is subjective, mere speculation, a welter of myth and poetry, religion and theology, magic and superstition. If systematized at all, they say, it is more deserving of the attention of the psychiatrist or, at best, the cultural anthropologist, than the serious student of ideas as such.[18] This judgement is untrue. One has only to understand the distinctions, and then one truly knows and understands. One has to be cautious all the time and avoid mistaking one thing for another, for superimposition *(adhyas)* is the root cause of suffering, and knowledge alone can bring about freedom from it. Shankara tried to make it very clear that the superimposition of the characteristics of not-self *(anatman)* on the Self, and vice versa, is the result of ignorance and the cause of all *maya.*[19] Instead of recognizing a rope, for example, for what it is, one sees a snake, instead. He is not only unable to perceive the rope, but he also superimposes a snake (perceived somewhere else in the past) onto it.

By the same token, if one understands the distinctions he can come to an understanding of that something which I call "X," and which is called by different names in different traditions of yoga. It is not only spirit as opposed to matter. It is not merely a "mystical experience," because it is "you" that is it, and you know that you are not merely a mystical experience. It is experiential, but it is not only "the experience" that is you, for the pronoun "I" or "you" designates more than substance, spiritual or whatever, or process even though there are some philosophers who take these pronouns to stand for processes only. It is unique, in a way, and maybe that is why it is called *anirvachaniya*—inexplicable. It is beyond predicates. But even though it is indescribable, those who experience it know it directly. The difficulty arises when they have to talk about it, for when we talk about it, we have to use language and concepts, and it cannot be captured through language and concepts. Is there another way? Yes, there is the way of the Upanishads:communicating through silence, or teaching through silence, or better still, communicating and teaching non-verbally. But let us not be misled by this process.

If one were to ask the best way to achieve *jnana*, Patanjali may be our guide: *abhyasa* (continuous, hard, arduous practice), and *vairagya* (non-attachment) are the two basic means. Follow whatever path is best for you. The tradition says that all of them are going to the same goal. One can make progress toward *jnana* with the help of all the yogas. Realization is the goal. It is the high value, for without realization there is no *mukti*—freedom. There may be a lot of other things, but there is no *mukti* without *jnana*. If final release is the goal, *jnana* is necessary. Otherwise one may rest satisfied on whatever level one has attained.

Jnana brings about the final release from the basic suffering that is caused by ignorance. The example given in the ancient tradition is that *jnana* is much like taking a thorn from your body. You feel relieved. So actually the goal is the complete relief and release that comes through Self-realization. Otherwise, even though the freedom is there, one does not know it. And if one does not know it, if one does not realize it, it is of no use to you. It is the *jnana* of what one is that matters most. Therefore, try always to seek the way to light from darkness, to knowledge from ignorance, and to emancipation and freedom from all suffering.

References

1. See Hiriyana, M., *Indian Conception of Values*, Kaivalya Publ, Mysore (India), 1975. p. 1. See also his early paper, "The Indian Conception of Values."

2. *Ibid.*, pp. 1-25.

3. Kaplan, Abraham, *The New World of Philosophy*, Vintage Books, pp. 199-228. Lecture on Indian philosophy.

4. See especially the Upanishads and the Bhagavad Gita.

5. The word *yoga* means *yoke, putting together, or harnessing our energies to realize the unity.* See Iyengar, Bk. 5, *Light on Yoga*, London, George Allen and Unwin, 1965, pp. 21-25.

6. For example, hatha yoga is especially related to the controlling of the body and *prana*, and that is included in the eightfold organs of raja yoga. Hatha yoga is thus a means to raja yoga. See *Hathayoga-Pradipika*, verse 2. Kevalam Rajyogaye Hathvidyopadishyate.

7. See Shankara Bhasya on *Vedanta-Sutra*, introduction.

8. See especially *Katha, Brihadaraynyaka* and *Mandukya Upanishads*.

9. Term *upadhi* is used to describe the accidental qualities. They are like titles, changeable, transitory and ephemeral. See also *Samkhya-Sutra*, 1.151-152.

10. *Chit* means *consciousness, matra* means *merely* or *only and nothing else*, hence the expression, *pure consciousness*.

11. See Shankara's commentary on *Vedanta Sutra*, introduction. He makes a distinction between self *(atman)* and not-self *(anatman)*. Ascribing the qualities of the one to the other is

called *adhyas* (superimposition). It is caused by mistakenly projecting something experienced elsewhere and present in the memory, to something else. When the qualities of any object are projected on the Self (subject) and an "appearance" *(maya)* is taken for reality, *ajnana* (ignorance) is the root cause.

12. *Ibid.*

13. Frequently it is declared in the tradition, *Jnate tattve kaha samsaraha.* There is no world of *maya*, of course, after the knowledge of reality.

14. See the fourth section of the *Yoga Sutras.*

15. See the *Katha Upanishad* for the analogy of the chariot.

16. The Upanishads say, *Vijnatarmare kena vijnaniyata.*

17. Kaplan, *op. cit.,* page 201.

18. *Ibid.*, p. 200.

19. See Shankara's commentary on *Brahmasutra*, introduction.

About the Writers

Sri Swami Rama—Born in 1925 in a learned Brahmin family in the Himalayas in India, Swami Rama was ordained a monk at a young age by a great sage of the Himalayas. In his early manhood, he was involved in a learning journey from monasteries to caves, studying and living with more than a hundred and twenty sages in the solitude of the Himalayan mountains and the plains of India.

From 1939 to 1944 he taught the Upanishads and Buddhist scriptures in various schools and monasteries in India. He then studied Tibetan mysticism from 1946 to 1947. In 1949 he became the Shankaracharya of Karvirpitham, the highest spiritual post in India. He renounced the dignity and prestige of this high office in early 1952 and returned to the Himalayas for final instructions from his Master before leaving for the West. For three years he studied Western psychology, philosophy and medicine in Europe. In 1970 he became a consultant at the Menninger Foundation in Topeka, Kansas, participating in experiments which revolutionized medical theories of the relationship between body and mind. Monitored on a battery of laboratory instruments, he demonstrated his ability to stop his heart from pumping blood for seventeen seconds and voluntarily maintained his production of various brain waves among many other scientific demonstrations of his yogic control.

In 1971 Swami Rama founded the Himalayan Institute of Yoga Science and Philosophy whose expanding educational and therapeutic work he continues to direct from its national headquarters in Honesdale, Pennsylvania, and its many centers throughout the world.

Swami Rama is the author of many books, including *Yoga and Psychotherapy, Lectures on Yoga, A Practical Guide to Holistic Health, Life Here and Hereafter* and *Living with the Himalayan Masters.*

The recipient of many honorary and service awards, Swami Rama was recently presented the Martin Buber Award for Service to Humanity.

Vasant V. Merchant, Ph.D.—Born in Bombay, India in 1933, Vasant Merchant received a Bachelor of Arts degree, a teaching diploma and a Masters of Arts degree from Bombay University. In 1957 she came to the United States where she became a teacher/counselor and researcher at the University of Minnesota. During this time she also received a second M.A. in Humanities. In 1963 she was awarded a teaching fellowship at the University of Southern California where she earned her Doctor of Philosophy in 1966. Dr. Merchant was Assistant Professor at the University of the Seas (World Campus Afloat) and from 1966 to the present serves as Associate Professor of Humanities at Northern Arizona University in Flagstaff, Arizona.

Her love for travel and research has made Dr. Merchant a specialist in twelve languages. She has lectured extensively to educational institutions and service organizations throughout the world and has received many academic and service awards for her efforts to bring an appreciation of the humanities to others.

Dr. Merchant is the author of *Religion and World Peace* as well as many articles on philosophy, music, and her great passion, the future of mankind as seen through the works of the great Indian seer, Sri Aurobindo.

Geshe Wangyal— After many years of intense study and practice of the Dharma in Mongolia, China and Tibet, Geshe Wangyal was given the title *Geshe* which indicates the attainment of the highest level of scholastic and spiritual knowledge. During his years of study, he received teachings from some of the most famous lamas of this century, himself having become a lama at the famous Drepung Monastery near Lhasa, one of the three great monastic centers of Tibet.

In 1955 Geshe-la came to America and founded Labsum Shedrup Ling (The Lamaist Buddhist Monastery of America) in New Jersey, the first Tibetan Buddhist monastery in this country. Since then Geshe-la has been a major force in the spread of Buddha's teaching in the West, teaching and lecturing on the history, theory and practice of Buddhism, and translating Sanskrit and Tibetan texts into English. He combines a great love of humanity with a profound knowledge of the ancient scriptures. Practical and loving, Geshe Wangyal uses all available methods to further the understanding of Dharma among Westerners.

In 1972 Geshe Wangyal founded the

Buddhist Studies Institute, a center dedicated to the translation of Buddhist texts, and the teaching, study and practice of the Dharma.

Munishree Chitrabhanu—At the age of twenty, Munishree became a Jain monk because he wanted to understand the meaning of life. His twenty-nine years as a monk were spent meditating and teaching, and walking barefoot over 30,000 miles through the villages of India. The Jain tradition emphasizes *ahimsa*, reverence for all life, and the practice of strict self-discipline. For five years he remained in silence.

In 1965 Munishree became one of the spiritual leaders of the Jains and founded the Divine Knowledge Society in Bombay which operates medical and famine relief stations and educational programs throughout India.

In order to address the Spiritual Summit Conference in Geneva in 1970, Munishree was the first Jain monk to break the ancient rules prohibiting the wearing of shoes and traveling by vehicle. As he became aware of the desire of Westerners for the teachings of Jainism, he made the decision to renounce the monastic life and to accept the many invitations to teach in America. Consequently he lectured at a wide variety of institutions of learning such as Sarah

Lawrence, Princeton, Cornell, the United
Nations, Koinonia Foundation, Pendle Hill,
Wainwright House and others. He worked
closely with the World Fellowship of Religions,
the Temple of Understanding, and other organizations.

Fluent in ten languages including Sanskrit,
and the author of nearly thirty books, Munishree now teaches and leads meditation at the
Jain Meditation International Center in New
York City and keeps an active schedule of
lectures across the country.

Bhagwan Bakhsh Singh, Ph.D.—A researcher and seeker of truth, Bhagwan Singh
holds Bachelor and Masters of Arts degrees in
Philosophy from Allahabad University in India
and a Doctor of Philosophy with distinction
from New York State University at Buffalo.
His dynamic lecturing on the philosophy and
practice of what he calls "scientific yoga" have
been enthusiastically received in several uni-
versities in India and across the United States.
He has been invited to address many international conferences and educational organizations on the topics of Indian philosophy and
religions and has written several books and
numerous articles on these topics. Dr. Singh is

currently Professor of Eastern and Western Philosophy and Religions at the University of Nevada in Las Vegas, and at Southern Illinois University at Carbondale.

HIMALAYAN INSTITUTE PUBLICATIONS